Binary Options

A High Probability Technical Blueprint for Success

(Most Profitable Binary Options Trading System & Powerful Money Management Strategies)

Harry Williams

Published By **Cathy Nedrow**

Harry Williams

Binary Options: A High Probability Technical Blueprint for Success (Most Profitable Binary Options Trading System & Powerful Money Management Strategies)

ISBN   978-1-7774403-4-3

Legal & Disclaimer

Table Of Contents

Chapter 1: Binary Options what exactly is the definition of a binary option?

It is an instrument of financial trade that is characterized by an agreed upon or guaranteed amount of money that can be paid out should the option expire in the cash, or in the event that the option

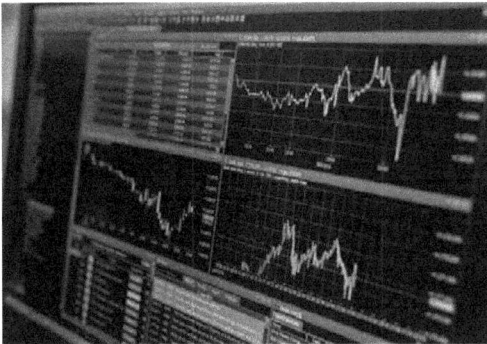

Expires without of money, the person trading it will forfeit the money they put into the option. The result of a binary choice is built on a straightforward "yes or no" concept, which is why it has its name binary option. The binary options have

expiry dates. When the expiry date is set the value of the underlying asset option has to remain on the upper side of the strike so that the trader can earn an income.

Courtesy of Pixabay

History of Binary Options

In 1971 in 1971, in 1971, the Chicago Board of Trade established the Chicago Board of Options Exchange also known as the CBOE it was the first designed platform for trading in options. After the establishment of the board, trading on binary options was not yet uniform however it was the first step towards the development of rules and standards in the following years.

Over time the improvements of the laws that were enacted, and a number of frameworks were designed to control the standard of options traded, and also to facilitate the expansion of the market in order to bring new buyers. The result was the establishment of OCC (The Option Clearing Corporation) to supervise the trade of assets and also to be empowered to enforce the utmost bans in cases that involved fraud or malpractice. This new guidelines helped to ensure greater efficiency in options, and improved the confidence that option trading engendered. The binary options market was steadily growing the interest of investors however they were still just a tiny portion of trades that were conducted.

In 2007 the OCC was granted permission to major stock exchanges the option of trading binary options. It was the US Securities and Exchange Commission (SEC) adopted this policy in 2007 and allowed the legalization of binary options that are all or nothing that could be traded as securities within the world's financial market. In May of 2008 The American Stock Exchange became the first exchange in the world to be open for trading binary options, and CBOE swiftly adopted the same policy. Binary options were offered were referred to as Fixed Return Options.

Although binary options are now accessible for all traders but they were initially thought to be a very complex and difficult instrument. Initially, the only options offered was call-based options. Once all changes had been implemented, binary options were made extremely well-known.

The initial change included the introduction of a variety of Binary options such as the creation of stocks options and the futures market, Forex, and such. Another change came with major enhancements to the platforms for trading and their websites to make it easier for the procedure of trading online. Implementation of stringent guidelines and rules by authorities that regulate the industry ensured that brokers as well as the platforms for trading were fair and honest when they dealt. Different regulatory bodies like those of the Cypriot Safety and Financial Exchange Commission have been established. Introduction of different binary trading platforms has opened market to traders across the globe to begin trading on binary options via the most suitable channel, which is online trading. Binary options are now trading all over the globe and are able to grab the interest of an audience which was formerly unaware of this tool.

The trading of binary options on websites is extremely appealing to traders across the globe. The foundational principle of binary options is the same, however, the technologies used to enable trading in them and the laws that govern them have changed dramatically due to their rapid rise in popularity.

In the beginning, technology was designed in order to provide investors with an online platform accessible on desktops however, in the latter half of 2013 when the access to these platforms was made available to mobile devices, too. It gave traders the ease of trading binary options anywhere around the globe. The technology behind the binary market is constantly changing, making it simpler for traders to trade on a variety of different assets across the globe, at their own convenience.

Since the regulations for binary trading, and also the technology behind them is changing, the top binary options brokers have begun to upgrade their platform in order to provide superior service for their customers. With the addition of a variety of international resources from all continents allows binary trading for traders all day long. Today, traders can almost trade 24/7. Brokers have also begun to offer different expiry times that permit traders to make an order in 60 seconds, one hour per day, week monthly, and even on a quarterly basis. Tools for trading online, such as the accessibility of comprehensive education centers, educational and informative videos, as well as regular and daily market reviews provide traders with the required data to help them take sound decisions when trading. Beyond that brokers have also begun adding different security features in addition to methods of payment that help traders trade more easily across the globe. These improvements throughout time have been a factor in the rise and recognition in binary trading.

Working of a Binary Option

Binary options are auto-exercised. This means either the gain or loss of the trade will be transferred or deducted directly from the account of the trader upon its expiration.

Like I said that a binary option relies on a no or yes idea. A binary option may be that is as straightforward as determining whether the value of XYZ Company will be more than $25 on the 25th of November at 10:10 a.m. A trader could choose to opt for the option of Yes (the price is higher) or no (the price will be less). Let's say that the trader believes prices are likely to go beyond $25 at the date and time and would like to place a wager of $100 for the same.

If the price of shares from XYZ Company increases beyond $25 at the specified date and time the trader will receive the amount that was calculated at the time of the transaction. We will assume that the amount paid was 70. Thus, in this instance, the trader has to gain $70 and that money is transferred to the account of the trader. If the gamble of the trader doesn't result in a profit, then the player will forfeit all the money he put into the bet, which is $100 in this instance.

What's the distinction between an option that is binary as well as a vanilla option? The vanilla option is an American option that grants its holder the ability to buy or sell the actual asset for a certain cost prior to the expiration of the option. An European option is also governed by this same principle, but the one difference is that a option holder can exercise this right only at the time expiration. Vanilla options are an ordinary option which gives traders the chance to eventually become the owner of the asset. If you buy these types of options, your chance of losing is limited.

However, your profits fluctuate in response to changes in cost of the asset.

Are binary options available to residents of the US?

They differ from binary options because they do not provide the possibility to combine any investment that is related to the actual asset. Binary options always provide two aspects: a maximum payout as well as an unassailable maximum risk which is only limited to the amount invested by the investor makes through said option. The payouts and loss will be affected due to the rate of progress or fluctuation of the actual asset. The proportion of the profits or loss is determined by whether the value of the asset in question is within the upper or lower end of strike prices, or it is not. There are binary options that can be shut down prior to expiration, however it will significantly decrease the amount of money that the investor will get from the option.

Sometimes the binary options can also be offered on platforms controlled by the SEC and various other regulating organizations However, most trading that is carried out in binary options typically is done outside of in the United States and may not be subject to regulation. Brokers that deal in binary options that aren't licensed cannot be held accountable for ignoring the strictest standards which is why all prospective customers must take care in dealing with brokers that are not regulated.

Image Courtesy of Pixabay

The US, Nadex is a authorized exchange for binary options. Binary options offered on Nadex depend on either or not propositions and offer traders the choice of removing the contract prior to expiration the cost that the binary option chosen is a sign of the possible profits or losses.

Let's suppose that an ABC company's share price is $64. This means that the strike price for the binary option is $65 and the option is scheduled to expire around 12 noon the next day (the most a person can stand to earn is $100 while the loss maximum is the investment amount). The trader is able to purchase the option at a price of $40 currently. If the option is successful, and the stock can end its trading at or above $65 before the option expires, then it has a value of 100 dollars. This means that traders stand to earn 60 dollars from the trade.

If the option expires, and its value is lower than $65 then in this case, the investor will lose the investment that was initially made ($40). If it is an Nadex Binary option the total of the possibility of profit and loss is always $100.

If the investor wants to make more money it is possible to alter the amount of options being exchanged. In the example above, if a trader chooses to put their money into three different options at the same time as per the instance, the highest risk of the investment will be $120 and the final profit is $180.

The non-Nadex binary options have a lot in common. Only difference is that they're not regulated by the US and don't offer the option of exiting prior to expiration. They don't offer an exact percentage of the payout or payout, and aren't offered in 100 increments.

Although there's been a huge expansion in binary options trading over the last few time, the idea is not a brand new idea. It's actually existed for some time in the past.

At the time of its launch, only financial institutions, investors with certain qualifications, as well as other traders with institutional status were the only people who had access to the binary option market. They typically performed over the counter and regulations were very minimal.

Chapter 2: Benefits of Binary Options

The binary option market has been gaining traction in the world of finance in the present. They are an excellent method to invest in various financial assets on a wide range of markets. Furthermore, they can provide a huge reward with a lower time-to-reward as compared with conventional investing. In this article I'll walk you through all the advantages you will profit from trading binary options.

Limited Risk

One of the greatest advantages of binary options is the fact that it doesn't require large amounts of money to invest in them, and you could do it using a limited amount of cash. This results in a lower chance of losing money when trading. The risk inherent in binary options is limited by the amount you are trading. Take this into consideration with the knowledge that on the majority binary options you're provided with details on what you are likely to win or lose prior to you make a decision to invest. This helps you plan for losses that could occur and allows you to make investments with the funds you have. In essence, you'll be capable of calculating the potential risk prior to investing one cent. It is a feature that binary options are the only ones that offer.

High Rewards

The time to expire for binary options typically are shorter contrasted with other traditional financial instrument or way for trading. The duration of the expiration ranges from 60 seconds up to a week. However, the traditional instruments are useful for longer time periods (it could be some months or even years before you get any type of income from these instruments). The quick return from trading coupled with extremely high returns (usually around 70 and 80 percent) can allow traders to create quick and profitable traders earn substantial profits.

Simple to Trade

To speed through the process of obtaining the first deposit that will allow for you to begin with binary options, the process is as straightforward as it is possible. There's only a couple of actions you'll need to follow such as choosing which financial asset you wish to trade as well as the amount you would like to invest, as well as the direction that you believe the price going to go. After that, you must choose the time of expiration time and then relax and then wait until the date of expiry. Just a couple of clicks and you're done. If the results of a particular trade prove beneficial to you, it is possible to make an enormous profit.

Less Investment

The binary options market allows traders to trade only tiny amounts at any moment in time and that is one of the advantages in binary choices. It is possible to begin trading with no worries about investing huge amounts of cash. Many brokers permit traders to place a trade for as little as $1. This gives the trader the option to trade as low or however much they want. At first, I'd advise you to stick with smaller amounts until you have the experience required to take larger trades. Be sure to don't trade anything more than you are able to risk.

An Array of Internationally Traded Assets

There are many different financial instruments that you could trade around the globe regularly. That means that whatever your preferred asset might be, or what your expertise in market is and how you can use them, you should be able choose them as the options you have.

Many binary options brokers offer a variety of kinds of financial assets let you trade, so make sure that you review them with care. Some brokers provide an array of commodity pairs, currency pairs as well as indices (up to 90 choices) so you'll choose the best options to trade.

Market Conditions

With regard to binary options, there's something that distinguishes these options from the rest of instruments that are conventional. With binary options, not only can gain a profit when price is rising however, you also have the chance to gain money when prices decrease. This allows for various trading strategies, and provides more opportunities for traders to profit. Also, any change of the market, no matter which direction it's heading it can assist traders in binary options earn an income (provided they make an appropriate bet).

Trade Anywhere

Nowadays, nearly everything we do are digitalized. Why does trading be any more different? Today, binary brokers are taking the lead to appeal to a digital market. This means that the majority of the platforms for binary brokers are online traders are completely free to trade anywhere around the globe at any moment in time. Furthermore, many websites are compatible with a variety of devices such as desktops computers, laptops and smart phones. That means you can make trades on the move and check the effectiveness of your choices wherever you are as well as in actual time. If you add this to the fact that all instruments are globally traded which means at the very least, one binary option exchange is always open anywhere across the globe. Therefore, you'll can trade these options all day long all week long. Options trading in binary do not have to be restricted by the hours that work for the exchange.

The numerous benefits binary options can provide are attractive. They're widely accessible easy to access and easy to invest in quick, and provide high return on investment, while not imposing a minimum limit on how much you invest. The above is why binary options are a fantastic tool for trading in the financial market. All you have to do is make sure that you're in charge before you begin taking advantage of the advantages.

Chapter 3: Binary Options Jargon You Must Know

What's the strike cost? What exactly does a call put option refer to? What exactly does "in the bank" means? Do you find yourself thinking that all this may seem Latin for you? But don't worry! I've got your back! In this article you'll learn more about the most important binary options terminology that you must be familiar with.

Image Courtesy of Pixabay

Call Option

The contract is between the buyer as well as the seller that grants the person who bought the call the option to buy the underlying financial asset an agreed upon time at a predetermined price. For simplicity an idea, a call option can be bought by investors who anticipate that the cost of the asset to increase prior to the date of expiry. If you opt for a standard option, the amount you can profit or lose is determined on the cost associated with the option, as well as on the movements of the market over the price of strike. Binary options are a different story. The trading risk of the trader is only the capital put into the option, and the gains are set by a set amount regardless of any movement in the asset in question.

Put Option: It's a contract between the buyer as well as the seller that gives the buyer the right of selling the asset at an agreed upon time and cost. Simply put the trader buys an option to put on in the event that they believe value of the asset is likely to fall below the strike value prior to expiration.

Underlying Asset or Instrument

The asset upon which the option was based is called the "underlying" asset. The most common examples of instruments that are underlying include commodities, currency pairs or stocks from which the option contract can be formulated.

At the Money

In essence, it is an instance where the strike price for an option is identical to the value of the asset that is being traded. As an example, suppose you purchase one S&P 500 option that has an expiration date of $1500 however, if that same option price is traded for $1,500 in the marketplace, the option will"ATM" (At the Money) "ATM" (At the market price).

Refund

If the money that the investor invests in will be returned to the trader because of an expires ATM. The situation is not common.

Out of the Money (OTM)

It's a scenario where the strike price for an option is greater than the cost of the contract that is underlying for the call option. This also applies to situations where it is lower than the value of the contract to purchase an option called a put. In the example above, suppose that S&P futures trade at $1500, a call option will be OTM in the event that the strike price is greater than $1500 and the strike price for the option lower than $1500.

In the Money (ITM)

This is a situation which all traders of binary options would like to have since it's profitable. In this scenario, that the price of the option is lower than the contract for the future's underlying price for a call or greater than the value of the contract for the future that is underlying for an option called a put. In the example above, if S&P futures trade at $1,500, an option with a strike value less and with a price higher than that can be profitable with a call as well as a put option and vice versa.

Payout

It's the percentage of investment return that is ITM.

Digital or Binary Option

The term refers to the option that has the risk of a fixed amount, and the payoffs depend upon whether the trader determines that an financial instrument on which the underlying investment is based will close higher (for the call option) and below (for an option to put) an exact strike price.

Strike Price

A price agreed upon and established at the start of the transaction which will decide if the buyer will end up with ITM or OTM at the time of expiration.

Expiry Date

The time that the option is due to expire could be as little as 30 seconds or some weeks.

Early Closure

You can choose to cancel an option before the expiration date. There are only a handful of brokers that offer this feature, and it could be a few fees due to an early closing.

Expiry Level

It is the value of the actual asset on the date of expiry. In the case of an example, if the expiry value is higher than the strike value for an option to call, the option will be ITM which means that the trader will be the money.

Market Price

This is the current rate that the investment is evolving within the market.

Chapter 4: Types of Binary Options

Each binary options broker is going to have a wide range of options. For traders with a variety of options, it can seem overwhelming, particularly in the event that you're not sure of what each one means. In the hope of being better than others, all brokers is trying to offer all the options that they can and they will also employ different names for the different options, even though they're all referring to identical things. In this article you'll learn more about the various types of binary options are available for trading in the marketplace.

Put/Call Options

They're referred to as call or put options or the options of high or low. It is by far the most widely employed form of options. Actually, it is the basis of binary options trading. The trader has to predict whether the value of the actual asset is going to be less or more than the established rate at a particular time in the near future. In this case, for instance, you could purchase an option that permits the possibility of earning profits within the hour, if the price of oil exceeds $100. You can also offer an option for sale and make an income in the event that the price for oil is lower than $100. The process is simple as it gets. The amount you receive will be determined by the broker. In the case of example, if the payout percentage is at 80 percent and, the event of loss, the payout is 10 percent, that implies that, when you buy an option that is worth $100, you'll receive $180 when the option is ITM or only $10 in the event that it's not ITM.

Binary options are so named since the payout relies upon only two possible outcomes - either the price increases or fall. The trader is paid only if the trader accurately anticipates the result. The purchase of a call option when you're certain that the value of the asset being traded is expected to rise. On the other hand, you would buy a put option if you believe that the cost is likely to decrease.

One-Touch Options

The requirements for these types of options can be managed. They're referred to as one-touch options by the majority of brokers, and can be a bit more complicated than the previous types of Put/Call options. There is no need for the trader to make a guess as to whether the cost will be higher or less than a certain price. If a single-touch option is used, traders must consider on whether the option will "touch or exceed" an exact price at the time expiration or it will not If the rate is greater than the current rate the option is considered called a call option However, If the price is not high and it's an option to put.

The type of investment provides an opportunity to pay out only when the value of the asset in question reaches an amount that is known by the term trigger. If it gets to the trigger point that the trader receives an amount. This option is suitable but only if the trader is confident that the asset is likely to show an extremely strong move in the direction chosen and it is likely to hit the trigger point regardless of whether a price rise is viable for the market or it is not. When you use these strategies that are available, the direction along with the trigger value, are fixed. The only thing you have to do is speculate as to whether the conditions be fulfilled or not.

If you sell an option to call, it is possible to earn profits only in the event that the rate stated by you does not get achieved. If you decide to purchase put options that you can profit from only when the rate that you specify has been reached or the reverse is true. It is possible to trade these options on weekends only. It is important to note that the "touch price" for the coming week is set over the course of the duration of the week. The options are gradually gaining recognition and are popular in markets that are volatile. This makes it more likely that the assets being touched or not touching an exact rate.

No Touch Options

An option that is not touched is the complete opposite to an option that is one-touch. The trader must bet that an underlying product will not achieve the price at which they have set. You or your broker must choose a price which is higher or less than current prices and then bet that it will not reach the level you have set at the time of expiration. If it is able to reach the price (even only once) and the contract becomes OTM and reverse.

They are extremely risky which is why the returns offered are large also. The amount of payout is contingent on the distance that is required to reach the trigger value. Touch, in addition to alternatives that do not touch, offer a an excellent payout due to the fact that the demands to be satisfied are harder to fulfill when compared with a normal put or call option.

One-touch options offer a greater payout when the trigger value is further from the present price. In the case of gold, for instance, if it is currently trading at $1300 an ounce right now, but the trigger for the option is $1,350 then the payoff is higher than that offered on an option with a trigger value of $1,320.

The option that is no-touch can yield a good return when the trigger price is more close to what is currently. Therefore, the payoff at a trigger cost of $1,320 is higher than a payout with $1350. The chance of hitting close to the goal is greater as is chances of being converted to OTM.

Double One-Touch Options

The reasoning that this choice uses is similar to the one-touch option. There is only one difference: the double one-touch option, there are two triggers - one for both sides of the current price. You can choose ITM in the event that the price of the instrument is able to break through one of the triggers you have set in any way, no matter which trigger.

In the example above, if gold currently trades at $1,300 but both you and your broker decide to set an upper trigger of $1,350 with the lower trigger is set at $1,280. Your option will be considered to be profitable if price goes up from $1,350 to $1,280. If the price does not reach either limit prior to the expiration date and the option is deemed to become OTM. This is a great option in the event of a market consolidation in which traders are certainty that price will rise and fall out fast however isn't certain of the direction in which it will move.

Double No-Touch Options

A double-no-touch option is based on the same reasoning as the no-touch option, which is the reverse of a double-touch choice. The trader is required to pick two triggers in order for the option be considered ITM, the price of the asset in question cannot exceed either trigger value prior to the expiration date. If the price of the asset exceeds one of the limit, the option will become OTM as the trader loses the money. The majority of traders select this choice when they're sure they will see the markets settle with a tight trading zone.

Paired Options

They are very exotic and only available through only a handful of brokers. They're based on the performance of the underlying asset, in comparison to an asset. A trader must select an asset pair from the list and then speculate on which one is more profitable than the other for the specified time. The assets are all placed in pairs based on their category as well as their sector. The selected assets have to come in the same class.

There are a variety of binary choices available. you should select the one that best suits your financial requirements.

Chapter 5: Risks Involved

While there are methods to lessen the risk taken by the vast majority of financial companies however, each investment comes with at the very least a certain amount of risk. This is the case for binary options. So, it is suggested that those who invest in this sector be aware of the different types of risks associated, and then take action so to make sure that the risk is to a minimum.

Types of Risks Involved

While there's no method to completely eliminate risks with every investment but having a thorough knowledge of potential risk can reduce the uncertainty for investors. This will help investors concentrate on the investment itself and identifying areas where there could be certain risks.

The risk that traders might face when trading binary options could be:

Risks in the market

Similar to other investment options like other investments, trading in binary options can be a part of the overall market risk. The majority of times the market can and frequently does, shift around without announcement. Though there are methods to forecast the future changes in the market but even the best analysis can't always pinpoint where the market is headed.

A fixed or limited amount of money earned

A further risk binary options traders need to be aware of is fixed profits. When investing in these types of investment, losses as well as profits are in a limited amount, which signifies that they are not able to grow infinitely in potential. In contrast there is a limit on losses.

Very precise profit and loss points

In addition, unlike other instruments of investment the binary option is measured using the lowest score. That means, typically the amount for this kind of investment is able to be determined using the decimal point of three or four places. In the case of binary options trading it is possible to use even 0.0001 points may be the variation between an option operator which can be on the other side of the investment gain or loss.

Not liquid

They are not classified as to be a "liquid" investment option. Since these types of instruments can't be used indefinitely the traders need to be patient and wait until the options expire before they are able to make either a loss or gain (unless it's the case with a Nadex binary option).

There is no ownership in the assets

Because binary options are an investment in the direction taken by the base asset, the operators don't make investments in tangible assets. Although many people are confident with this kind of investment, a few be concerned about the danger.

Regulations on scarcity

One of the most significant dangers of trading binary options is the fact that online trading platforms aren't yet regulated. So, even if the majority of Binary options trading platforms may be exactly as they seem it is possible that the traders could face certain types of unethical practices.

How Much Should You Risk Per Binary Options Trade

Binary options can be described as an "all or none" type of option in which the trader is required to risk a certain amount of money and can be able to lose that capital or gain an undetermined amount of money based on the fact that the value of the underlying instrument is higher or below a certain price at a certain time. If the trader is able to predict correctly it will be paid the amount of money that was set. In the event that he they are wrong, the investor loses all the capital that he or she wagered. The definition of "fairness" was greatly extended when the American-based Nadex introduced options that allowed traders to either buy or sell the option at anytime time until expiration. It created many situations since traders can quit with less than amount of profit or loss.

Whatever binary options that you use, whether Nadex or conventional binary options, your position size matters. The position size determines the risk you take on the trade. What you decide to put at risk should not be arbitrary nor depend on whether you believe that a particular trade would be beneficial for the trader or not. It is necessary to have a position size formula you can apply in all transactions.

What is the maximum amount you put at risk with one option trade? It should only be a tiny portion of the total capital you invest in trading. You can decide the percentage you want to risk, however it's not recommended to take on more than five percent of your money. Indeed, professionals are careful not to take on greater than 1 percent of their capital.

If, for instance, you've got $1,000 in your account, you should reduce the risk by one or two percent ($10-20) for each trade made using binary options. The most risk you are able to take is five percent, or $50.

Anything greater than that shouldn't be considered. Once you begin trading with a broker, you'll be looking to make the most money as quickly as you can. The idea of making a quick cash can be tempting however, you shouldn't succumb to this urge. If you take a risk for each trade you take and you are a risk, you could be unable to fund your account until you get a huge windfall. Many newbies aren't using an approach to trading that has been tested and proven; rather they choose to go with the flow the process. It's best to put a portion of your money on every trade, to test strategies for trading as well as develop your skills. If you're advancing, you'll be able to gradually the amount you risk to approximately 2 percent.

How can you calculate the probability of a loss on a trade? Options that are binary always come with an established maximum risk. The risk provides you with an estimate of the amount that you'll lose in the event the actual asset fails to perform in the manner you anticipated. When it comes to binary options, the risk is the cash you place on a bet.

If you place a bet of the sum of $10 on a trading transaction, you will lose $10. loss. There are brokers who offer refund on trades that fail. If, for instance, the rebate amount is 10 for example the maximum loss you can incur would be $9.

Maximum loss + Rebate = Trade Risk

$10 + (10% of $10) = $9.

The Nadex binary option isn't able to provide a refund in the event of a trade that is unsuccessful. However, if you buy an option for $50 and the cost drops to $30, it is possible to sell the option for a fractional loss rather than waiting to see a decrease in price until it is zero or for it to rise by more than $50. After expiration the

Nadex option is valued at 100 or nothing. When taking a risk assessment it is important to consider the possibility of a worst-case. Every Nadex options can trade between zero and 100. Each digit represent one dollar worth of profits or losses. If you buy an option worth $30 and the price falls to zero, the loss will be $30. If you buy an option at 50 but the price reaches 100, the loss will be $50. There are multiple options to trade in order to maximize your profits.

What are the steps to determining the amount of money you will need to invest in the binary option trade? Now you know how much you're willing to gamble in a trade, as well as what you stand to be losing in the course of a trade. The next step is to add those two factors together in order to figure out what amount you could be wagering in a binary option.

In the example above, if your account is worth $3500 and you're putting two percent for each trade, your maximum loss is 70 dollars. If the broker does not offer an incentive for losing trade, make sure you do not risk greater than $70. If it happens that the broker is willing to offer 10% rebate then you could be able to risk up to $77 ($70 plus rebate). If you lose then you'll receive the rebate of 10 percent and the loss you incur is not more than $70--2 percent of your account balance.

When making trades with Nadex binary options there's additional step that needs to be taken since it is possible to purchase options for any price that is that is between zero and 100. It also impacts the risk you are willing to risk losing. If, for instance, you own $5,500 in your account, you could be liable for two percent per transaction. This means you could be losing $110 on each trade, while still being within the risk ratio you want to be. Do not invest in a deal that could result in losing more than that sum.

Let's say you want to purchase an option of gold binary options. You believe that the price of it is likely to rise today. You make the decision to buy the option for 50. If your prediction is correct and the price of gold exceeds what the strike price is at the time of expiration and your contract expires, the option is valued at 100. The possibility of making an income of $50 from every contract you purchase. If the value at closing is lower that the strike value on expiration this means that the option is worth nothing that is, you will be liable for $50 per contract. Therefore, you risk $50 per trade that you enter. Your risk tolerance is $100 per trade. This means you could buy two $50 contracts. If you lose, your loss would be

$100. This remains within the risk limits If you purchase three contracts the total risk will be $150. it is greater than your tolerance for risk.

Tips for Trading in the Real World When you're getting your feet wet You must determine the ideal size of your position to each trade you execute. If you're a day trader you'll need time to calculate the maximum amount of money you are willing to risk depending on your tolerance to risk and then make trades accordingly. This easy step will benefit you in the long run, and if you fail to win money, you will lose the amount of money you could be able to afford (on declining value of your account) If you do win, the amount you risk increases (the value of your account increases). The only thing that is in place regardless of value of the account is the proportion of risk.

When your account begins to improve, it is possible to begin trading with the same amount for each trade. In the case of example, if your amount of your account remains stable, you'll be able to take your profit towards the end of the month. In addition, any fluctuations in your balance could be fixed quickly with two or three profitable trades. Thus, it is not necessary alter the size of your position for every trade you take. If the value of your account is set at $5,000 and you are able to risk 2 percent on each trade, the risk is fixed at 100 dollars per trade. Try not to raise or decrease the risk by more than a couple of dollars every time the balance of your account is over or below the mark of $5,000. This is to ensure that you do not take on more than one or 2 percent of your account to ensure that you don't make a loss of 100 or fifty trading sessions per week before emptying your account.

This is a decent degree of protection that a beginner can maintain.

Being able to change the size of your position continuously for each small change in your account's value lets you make fast trading decisions even when the market is extremely volatile. If you are aware you are able to risk anywhere from $10 100 dollars on a trade, you could cut down on time by acting immediately, instead of considering the risk of risking either $105 or the equivalent of $95.

Here's a short summary of everything that was discussed within this chapter.

The first thing you need to make is to make sure you have a risk percentage that is fixed. Keep it at 1 or 2 percent or, at a minimum, five percent and no higher than five percent. In a typical binary options trade, this figure will give you the highest risk. In the case of the Nadex binary options, you must take into consideration your highest risk for the transaction and determine the quantity of contracts you could execute within the amount.

At first, it is essential to determine the size of your position on each trade you execute. This is an excellent ability that can prove useful. When your account is stable then you are able to continue using the same account.

Take care to calculate your risks, and resist your urge to increase the risk.

Chapter 6: Binary Trading Myths

There are a myriad of misconceptions surrounding trading with binary options. They are able to confuse and deceive an untrained or novice trader. The myths don't aid beginners learn how to trade and help them make money. Many of them have to do with regulations as well as trading platforms, while some relate to strategies for trading. One of the most untrue myths in all of them is not having unrealistic expectations of trading. In this part you'll learn about some of the most common myths regarding binary options, and also the truth.

Myth 1: It Isn't Legal to Trade

One of the most popular myths that many individuals think is that it is illegal to deal in binary options within the United States and that it is unlawful to trade binary options. I want to assure you that it is just an absurd belief. Allow me to invite for the

Commodity Futures Trading Commission or the U.S. CFTC to bust the myth of this:

David Meister, the director of the CFTC has stated that "It is unlawful to ask US individuals to purchase and trade commodity options, regardless of whether they're prediction contracts, unless they're listed as trading instruments and trading on a platform which is registered with CFTC or are legally exempt."

In simple terms It is permissible to deal or trade in binary options within the USA provided that these conditions aren't broken:

The brokerage you're working with is situated in the US the broker is accredited by the CFTC or handles any commodities that are legally exempt. It is true that many of the brokers that are regulated aren't able to offer binary options for US customers and this is the cause of the myth among novice traders that they can't trade binary options inside the US.

Myth 2: It's a Scam

On the other hand, there is a large number of novice traders who are wrongly believing that they are not able to trade binary options. On the other hand, there are plenty of prospective traders who believe that trading binary options is fraudulent or should not invest in binary options. They also believe that all other forms of trading also are frauds. What is the source of this absurd legend come from? It seems to me that there are two main sources where this myth originates: con artist brokers as well as naive traders.

It is a bit of a pity to state that con artists brokers are out there, and there are a lot of them operating in the financial world. They aren't reputable business people the only reason for them to exist is to swindle the money of your clients. They'll try their best to cheat you out of profitable trades. They will hinder your ability to access your cash as well as take your personal information. In order to deceive the victim, they pretend to be legitimate binary option traders. They're nothing but fraudsters, and be cautious when selecting an online broker. Learn more about how to choose a reliable broker by reading this guide.

The other issue concerns trading with naive traders. There will be traders who will spend their money trading with no regard to who they're doing trade with or the activities they're engaging in. Insufficient information is the most significant reason for the naiveté of traders. They're too ignorant and a bit foolish, and are an easy target to prey on. These traders think they are able to earn a lot of money overnight, with no knowledge of what markets do and what instruments they deal with. These traders appear to be relying on many of the myths that are discussed in this section. In essence, they set themselves up to be scammed. When they are unable to pay then they claim to others that they have been taken advantage of. This is why other traders will believe that they've been victimized by a scam. But the real problem is that they didn't invest enough time and energy absorbing the details of the financial market before they jumped right into investing.

Let me assure you that trading binary options isn't fraudulent. It's as legal as other methods of trade. All you have to understand is the way binary options work, locate an experienced broker and remain cautious when you make an investment choice. If you follow these steps then you're good to take the plunge.

Myth 3: A Demo Account isn't Important

Do you really need to spend your precious time using virtual currency before you can begin trading on the actual market? This is as you're only starting out, despite having done a lot of studies; the only thing you've got is your theoretical knowledge without any practical experience. Theoretically, something could look good but until and until you've tried the waters yourself it is unlikely that you'll know which methods work and what don't. Beginning with money that is real, in the absence of any prior previous experience, is akin playing. Instead of losing the money you have earned you should take time time to practice using the demo account. The loss of fake cash will not hurt you and even if you make few bad choices the experience will be an opportunity to learn. This may seem like an arduous process, but it's the most efficient and the most reliable way to get a better understanding about what you'll need to be doing. This will also help that you are patient and shrewd, two vital abilities you require to be a successful trader. It is my opinion that having a demo account is crucial. If you're new to the financial world, make sure that you have spent time time studying the manner in which the financial system works with an account that is demo.

Myth 4: You Need a Large Account

Another myth that is widely circulated is that you can't begin trading from a modest account. Did you hear that to begin trading, you'll require a couple hundreds or thousands of dollars? This is actually an untruth, and was based on fact which was distorted in the course of. If you adhere to the best practices for managing money, you'll realize that you only have to be risking a fraction of your money on each trade you execute (about 3 percent).

Therefore, you won't earn a lot of profit if you begin your account with just few hundred dollars however that's just a stage.

In time, your bank account will begin to grow through your choices in trading. Then, you will reach the point where even 3 percent can be a massive amount. Therefore, the main question is if you're patient enough to open a new account, and gradually work progress to larger trading. If yes, there's no reason to think that it is not possible to begin trading with a an account that is small. It's best to be safe and start with a small amount. Do you remember that tale about the tortoise & the Hare? A steady and slow pace wins the race. It is possible to apply this concept when trading. It is much more manageable than one that is a big risk for at least the beginning, until you have an understanding of what you do.

Myth 5: Trading Bonus is Free Money

Advertising such as "Get $300 in cash for making a payment now with the XYZ binary broker!" are quite common and everywhere on the web today. These ads constitute the main marketing strategy for many of brokers. Newbies are conditioned to believe that they'll receive the sum by simply opening an account with an agent. If you take the time to read through the terms and conditions, then you'll see that when you accept an offer, you are making a contract to turn over. If you aren't able to convert the amount of the bonus in increments of 20-40 times then you can't take the bonus promised to you. You are able to use the bonus for trading however; you cannot use it in any other way, in the event that you do not meet the requirements. There are several concerns with this type of arrangement.

It's always risky trading leverage. This means you'll likely be investing more than you are able to the risk. Additionally, it may be challenging to take any profits when there's the bonus amount. Therefore, it's crucial to understand the fact that bonuses are an incentive to trade, and there's no something as free money. It is up to you to decide whether all the hassles for benefit of a small bonus is worthwhile or not.

Myth 6: Perfect System = 100% Success

There is no other story more destructive than this. This is among the most frequently used phrases scammers can employ to swindle a skeptical investor. There is a possibility that they could promise a 100% or even 90% chance of success or even thousands of dollars an hour, but regardless what they're using is to capitalize on the notion that novices have--"the ideal strategy or approach to defeat the system." There's not anything that can be described as a "perfect" method to deal with the financial market. They are extremely unpredictable, and their volatility depend on a myriad of external influences which are impossible to anticipate the future of what could or won't take place. Each financial instrument comes with specific risks associated with they, and that applies to binary options also. It is possible to do certain things to limit the risk you take but it is impossible to entirely eliminate the risk. Anybody who claims that they will provide you with an unrisky trading strategy will lie to you. Avoid such individuals.

Myth 7: Earn $1,000 per Hour

It's not easy, but isn't difficult. It is not necessary to concentrate on the amount of income you will make in just an hour, or even dream of being a millionaire in few months. What you should be focusing on is that you should concentrate on is beginning to earn profits that are steady and stable. If you begin with an account that is small your gains may be minimal at first. Be prepared for the possibility that you earn only $10 one hour. One thing is important to keep in mind to keep in mind is that if are able to keep earning these profits consistently and you eventually arrive at a point when you earn $1,000 an hour. But it's not something that will be achieved in a single day, so you must be cautious. The business of dealing with financial instruments doesn't mean getting a quick cash flow If that's the only reason you trade or invest in, you should rethink the goals you have set. The goal is to create the long-term plan of action which will allow you to reap incredible profits.

Myth 8: You can trade up to 20% of your account

This is a random amount, however it's huge, in fact. It is not recommended to trade greater than 3 to 5 percent for each of your binary options you trade. Every successful trader knows there's a amount of risk as well as a losing streak not unusual. If you take on a risk of 20% or greater than that for five transactions, you could virtually empty your account in very little time. In general always avoid investing greater than the amount you be losing. It is impossible to predict how the market will turn downwards, which is why it's best to remain cautious in your investment decisions.

Myth 9: Always Rely on Your Gut

Some people think they have an extraordinary ability to forecast the direction of the stock market and other financial instruments. They believe they possess an intuitive sense of the market, or another mystical connection only they have the capacity of knowing. Such a belief gives them the illusion of safety. There may have been an unlucky streak and it could be over at any time as it does not really have anything to do with the ability to discern. Since trading on financial instruments aren't one to bet on.

So, let me explain the issues to those of you. There is no mysterious connection to financial markets. At times it's a great option to follow your intuition, however it doesn't mean you should do not pay attention to the numbers or facts. Binary options carry a certain danger that comes with them If you don't take care and take a risk, you could risk losing all of your assets. Be aware that the gut may, sometimes, become quite as volatile as the market itself, and that's just about as far as this link can get. It's better to adhere to a set of strategies and figures if you are looking to minimize your risk exposure.

Myth 10: Most Binary Options Traders Win

There is a chance that you've been conditioned to believe that traders who trade binary options are an active group of investors just like you. And they make a living through trading. It is possible to believe that many of them quit their job and embarking on the life of prosperity and excitement. Many of you believe that is true, however the truth is very different. In reality, just a tiny fraction of the tens of thousands of traders are able to generate a steady stream of earnings through this. This isn't a huge number however if you wish to live a lavish life similar to the majority, it is important to know some things. The key is to recognize that the wealth was accumulated wasn't a quick fix and it required a lot of time, effort and determination and the skills which they acquired to achieve their current level Currently at. There is no quick fix to successful life, which is true for trading too. If you're not careful and you don't take your time, you could loss more than you make.

Myth 11: Not as Profitable and Quite Risky

It is merely an untruth. If you manage your money correctly, then the binary option is more profitable than other methods to trade or invest in the markets for financial instruments. This is due to the fact that the return the binary options provide in terms of a percentage per transaction is greater than the one offered by option in the stock market.

Additionally the binary option is safer than investing in stocks. If you're trading stocks, it is necessary to place greater sum of money than what you would for binary options. In addition, the profits you are able to earn are greater than stock prices as well. With binary options, you are able to make a smaller investment and decide whether to forecast the future growth or decline in the value of your investments or you do not.

Myth 12: They're an Urban Legend

I'm not sure why people believe that making money through binary options is just a myth. This isn't true and it's a fable. Binary options trading were made accessible to everyone over the last few years Prior to that it was accessible only to traders with high power, those that are extremely skilled. The binary options used as the best of trading instruments, and only accessible to elite traders. When the door was made accessible to all many people have made huge amount of money from the alternative.

Myth 13: They Aren't a Reliable Tool

There is no evidence to suggest that binary options aren't trustworthy similar to other options in the market. They offer the chance to make extra income due to their dependability. Binary options represent the highest pay-out option, with the lowest cost of investment. A couple of thousand dollars investments on the market is reduced to just a couple of hundred dollars if you decide to trade on binary options. Thus, it's safe to conclude they are an excellent investment opportunity. There's no other tool in the marketplace that lets to achieve the levels of profit or flexibility that binary options offer.

Myth 14: Difficult to Understand

But this isn't the case. There are many individuals who are using binary options and do it successfully. There is a good chance to earn lots of additional income by working using binary options. The only thing you have to do is invest some time to learn the way these options operate in the first place. Everything you learn in this publication will aid you to understand this procedure.

Myth 15: They're a Waste of Money

This is wrong. In the past, I've mentioned the investment with binary options is less investment capital than a position on stocks. When you invest in binary options, you won't need to pay less than a few dollars for each investment. In contrast, you'll have spent hundreds of dollars for certain stocks, and the yield is much less. In addition, if you lose money in the market for stocks and you end up making a huge hole within your pockets. If you are unable to make money from binary options, then you do not have much to lose since it's not a huge investment at all.

Myth 16: Only Amateurs Trade in Binary Options

As I said in the earlier paragraphs the trading of binary options was previously limited to professionals the ability to make trades with these instruments unless you were employed by a large brokerage company. This instrument became available to everyone since binary options performed very exceptionally. The platform was designed by experts but it was designed in the hopes of assisting professionals. However, it is a bit absurd to believe that only amateurs can use the instruments. There were many professional traders who had already been dealing with these instruments long before anyone else could access them.

There are many who think that by investing using binary options, one could lose all of your capital. It's not true, and let me reiterate it that these instruments are more secure that any other offered on the stock market. Certain traders who deal in binary options aren't able to deal more than a couple of dollars in an time and no over that. They don't need to acquire stocks at a price that is exorbitant or notice a change in their margins of profit in a matter of minutes instead of waiting several weeks or days for a time.

After having gone through all of the lies in this section, I'm certain you've probably transformed your views about the binary option trading.

Chapter 7: Are Binary Options and Day Trading Similar?

In the case of trading, many people make use of a language that is not their own and assume that binary options and trading are synonymous. The truth is that a majority of mentions of binary options are to suggest that they're superior to day trading, or the fact that lots of trading day-traders "switch" to binary option trading. This causes confusion for novice traders who may think that day trading is somewhat untrustworthy and speculation-based and that binary option is safer and saner. Trading in binary options could be considered the day trader. Day trading only refers to the time period of trading.

Image Courtesy of Pixabay

Types of Trading

If you intend to invest with stock options, binary options, Forex, or any other type of instrument, you'll need to set up an time period in which you wish to make trades. When traders can choose to trade on a range of time frame, the majority prefer long or short-term trading and are able to concentrate exclusively on one aspect. These are the most common forms of trading according to your time frame.

One of them is trading in position or for long-term durations. This means that the trader will be in the market for a long time, whether it's weeks or months and sometimes even for years. Binary options allow you are able to become an option

75

trader should you want to and in the event that your broker allows the option of an extended duration time. Trading that runs for more than a week are termed longer-term transactions. If you make trades within this time interval regardless of the currency that you trade on, you're not trading as a day-trader.

The other is called an the inter-day trade, also known as swing trade. There is no way to be trading on a daily basis if you decide to go with this choice. A swing trade is an investment where the trader is in a position for a few days, typically from one to four days.

The other is intraday or day trading. When trading intraday it is the case that the trader holds the position for less than one hour. In essence, you'll be able to open and close trades within the same day. It is possible to hold the trade for just a few minutes or two or even days. It is possible to do this when trading with binary options, or any other financial instrument. The trade could end in sixty seconds, or perhaps twelve hours and remain a day-trade.

Why is Day Trading Considered Less Reliable?

The day trading market has the reputation of being more speculation-based than other types of trading. But do you believe it? It's likely to be the case. There's absolutely no reason one should think the possibility that holding a position only for a limited time is not as effective as an investment that is long-term. There aren't any inherent characteristics in day trading that render it less trustworthy as long-term or swing trading.

So, why do we have widespread beliefs that binary option trading is superior to trading on a daily basis? Let's for now forget that binary trading can be the day trader and we should rethink the concept of long-term as well as shorter-term trading in light of their advantages and negatives.

Benefits of Long-Term Trades

The long-term approach gives traders greater time to take a choice. This can be beneficial when you are unable to think fast under stress or require longer time to think about a choice. It is more difficult to drain the account of this kind of trade. If you notice something not going as planned the more likely to be aware it in time prior to wasting funds.

Disadvantages of Long-Term Trades

If you're given lots of time to reflect, there is a greater chance of having second thoughts about your choices. If you are prone to analyze or re-evaluate your choices regardless of whether you have made the right decision, it may cause you to be in trouble.

Benefits of Short-Term Trades

This means you'll be able to take advantage of more opportunities for trading. This is an excellent choice for those who are intuitive and do not have the time to sit and wait for lengthy trading sessions. If you are prone to doubting yourself, then trading on the short term can be a great alternative.

Disadvantages of Short-Term Trades

If you're not a fan of the notion of doing too much quickly, this isn't the right choice for you. These are not the best option for those who is unable to make a decision in a hurry. They're susceptible to more risky mistakes and instabilities along with technical issues. Any delay even a fractional one during the transfer of your order could cause you to lose a lot of money. It is possible to loss a significant amount of cash when you trade in a mere 60 seconds. There is a chance that you will blow your balance without realizing the fact that you have done. If you open an account that has a minimum account balance with a binary option brokerage and select 60 second trades, you could completely empty your account in several hours, or maybe just a few minutes.

Choosing Your Expiry Times

Then, how do you determine if day trading is the best option for you? Should you opt for a long-term trading strategy using weekly expiry time frames or is a more short time period suitable for your needs (minutes or hours)? When you looked through the advantages and drawbacks of both short- and long-term trades did you connect with one of the issues discussed? Consider your own personality as a trader and observe the way that it affects your choices. Are you worried that you'll be unable to sustain the long-term investment? Do you feel the pressure is too to much? Will you collapse or flourish in the face of the pressure? Do short-term trading affect your ability to make decisions and cause you to feel overwhelmed? Take your time to analyze the situation.

If you're just starting out with trading and aren't certain of what to do I've got a few of my tips.

Test back-testing a trading technique based upon historical data. Back testing is the process where a trading method is applied on historical data to determine whether the strategy worked at the time of implementation. It is also possible to experiment with a variety of strategies until you discover one that you are happy with. Certain methods have specific time frames, while others are suitable for different time frames. If you come across a strategy that is compatible with different times of trading, you can test the trades in various time periods and then see how you think regarding trading.

If you are trying to choose the ideal time interval, the ideal strategy is to try a demo. It is easy to understand how your feelings are portrayed regarding trading, as well as how trading of longer periods can mitigate these.

If you're confused and are unsure, consider trading on interdays. It is an ideal place to begin by if you wish to steer clear of extreme position in trading. Interday trading can help you get used to trading quickly, as well as help keep your emotions in check over long durations. When you are comfortable with the concept that you are getting, you may switch to a slow or more rapid time to

expire time according to your
requirements.

In the end, it's entirely dependent on you
whether you'd like to become trading on a
daily basis or not. There is a possibility of
being an option trader in binary trading
and day trader. It is also possible to
become a binary trader, without being a
day trader. Try these options out and find
the best option for your requirements.

Chapter 8: Binary Options Strategies

Why Do You Need a Plan?

The most important aspect to consider in every new venture you are looking to launch is having a clear program for the project to be completed. How is trading distinct from other endeavors you have ever undertaken? An effective strategy for trading should outline the goals you intend to achieve and why you are making it happen. The strategic plan is an assessment of your capabilities as well as the skills you have, the available resources, as well as your goals. It will act as a guideline that can aid you to come an investment plan which is profitable.

An effective trading plan will assist you to understand the "what" as well as the "why" which got to trading at all. It can assist you to define the steps that you should consider when evaluating, performing and managing your investments. There is a need to contemplate a few aspects before you develop the strategy you will use to trade. Have you got an established method? Are you clear on the motive that you are looking to make a trade? What defines success according to you? How will you achieve your objectives? Through the right strategy it is possible to accomplish these goals.

Although, having a trade plan doesn't mean you will succeed. It is essential to be competent enough to develop one that can assist you understand your motives and objectives, and then apply it to succeed with your investments. What is an effective trading plan, and what can it do to help when trading binary options? In this article we will discuss the significance of a trading strategy as well as the process of formulating your strategy for trading.

There's a distinct difference between being reactive and proactive. If you have a plan of action in place for investment, you'll be able to be sure to be more proactive than being reactive. Your future can occur instead of watching for it to come about. It's no longer necessary to endure the burden of circumstance. It's difficult to predict every change that markets can undergo; however, you won't need to be concerned over being caught unprepared in the event that you have a strategy to be in your place. Prepare for any eventualities and reduce the amount of damage could be incurred. If you've developed a strategy plan, you'll be aware of how you should react should things not turn in the direction they should have. There will be an understanding of the direction to take.

What is the difference between a decent and excellent idea? With no clear picture of what you are trying to accomplish and the purpose to do it, anything will appear to be a great concept. What do you want to do and what will your money be worth? Being clear about the goals you're trying to achieve and what you'll need to do will assist you in making more efficient use of your resources including the three most crucial assets you have at hand: your time as well as your effort as well as your money. It will allow you to take a more informed decision, instead of an emotional one. Impulsive decisions might not always pay you well. The use of a strategy to trade will aid in reducing risks. You cannot avoid the risk completely; however you will be able to minimize the risk you take through planning. This will aid to increase your profits.

One thing you must keep at heart when planning your investment is that you must understand that patience is an essential quality. Investments may not earn immediate profits, so take your time. Your hard work will surely be rewarded, even if not right away, but eventually.

Before beginning by establishing a plan of investment, you'll have be aware of a few aspects.

What are you hoping to achieve? Are you looking to begin investing in order to gain better financial control? Are you looking to earn extra income? Do you wish to establish an emergency fund to cover a future rainy day or retirement? The way you define what you'd like to accomplish will impact the decisions you make regarding investing. When you've figured out the motivating factor then the next thing to do will determine your degree of risk-taking. Are you averse to taking risks or are you afraid of risk? Do your attitude towards the risk of taking a chance influence your investment decisions? How does taking on risk impact other areas of your day-to-day life? After you've figured all of this and are able to determine the best course of action, the following stage is to determine the obstacles which stand in the way. Most of the time, one of the most significant challenges that you will face could be the issue of a time stress. Other challenges could arise such as a lack of resources or lack of knowledge.

Three Types of Strategies

The best way to decide is using your intuition but you do not require any trading strategies. However should you wish to succeed as a trader, this type method will not be beneficial. This could have the reverse impact. If you are looking to become a profitable and successful trader, then you require an option trading strategy that is binary. There are three types of strategies that each trader requires in order to succeed. They are according to.

Trading Strategies

There are two main motives to follow the rules of trading. It reduces the risk of taking emotional or irresponsible decisions in trading. Instead, it permits users to use preset guidelines that are based upon rationality and apprehension. A second benefit is that having a strategy for trading can help you benefit by repeated use. Without a plan for trading it is difficult to figure out what went well and what was the reason. Although you may be able to find those answers, it'll impossible to replicate exactly the same. The use of a trading plan helps make sure that trades remain based on logic and sensible thinking, while also ensuring you're aware of the patterns you are able to repeat, study and then adjust.

In this case, you could evaluate a certain strategy by making a set amount of transactions or following the end of a specified time interval. Does the strategy work? Do you earn good profits? Perhaps the method is helping you make money, but you're not earning as much as you'd hoped. In this case it is possible to see if your method's profits will grow in the future as well as make some changes to the plan to boost your profits. This can be done only in the event that you've a trade plan in the first place.

In the absence of a proper strategy for trading can lead to trading that is not just random and difficult to improve. With no strategy to trade established regardless of a predetermined amount of transactions or time interval, you are unable to assess your progress as you do not have something to gauge it against. What do you do in the event that you are unable to recover your funds? The only thing you can do is think about making more informed decisions in the near future, but there will be nothing that you can base any decisions upon. This is true even when you earn income, however it's not the amount you had hoped to earn. This is true regardless of whether you do make a profit, but you aren't capable of discern the method employed to earn money but you are unable to replicate the exact strategy. Each transaction is a separate trade and does not form part of your general strategy. This isn't a sensible method of trading.

Let's consider a situation that you don't possess a strategy for trading. In this scenario it is possible to earn 50% profit in the first month, and lose 50 percent in the following month. What can you do to determine the reason why one month has been more successful over the next? What will help you to figure out the adjustments is required? There is no way to make sense of all this.

Money-Management Strategies

Many people appear to commit the error of creating the idea of a trading plan without any other considerations. The strategy for trading helps you determine what kind of asset you'd like to trade as well as the total risk exposure. There is little or no consideration put into managing your money. An effective money management strategy can assist you to optimize your cash flow to help you beat any streak of losing and maximize your capacity to make money.

Let's take a look at an investor who does not have a strategy for managing money. The trader makes the decision to place 10% of his account's funds on every trade. If a trade is unsuccessful and he loses money, he'll need to gain 20 percent in order to make up the loss, and even break even. If a trader is losing three consecutive times for breaking even traders must earn an additional profit of 30 percent. It is evident that this is a very easy process and losing streaks could completely drain your account in a short time. If you have three failed trades one loses 30% of his account balance. If you consider the fact that many losing streaks run for more than three trading sessions you will come to recognize how important managing your money is.

If you don't have a strategy for managing your money your account balance could quickly be depleted regardless of whether you've got the right trading strategies put in place. The loss of streaks, along with trading that are not profitable, is a element of the trading. Therefore, if you've got an approach in place, then you'll be more prepared to handle these inevitable events. By focusing on the proper management of money, you'll be in a position to maximize the profits you earn, minimize your losses and be able to regain a profit in the aftermath of a bad patch.

Analysis and Improvement Strategies

In the realm of trading binary options There isn't a one that is the ideal method. Markets never stop evolving and successful traders have to be on top of their game and keep trying to improve, upgrade and improve their strategies for trading. Even veteran traders have to examine and refine the ways they trade to remain profitable. This is the case for novice traders, too.

A strategy for analysis and improvement offers the trader a logical way of enhancing the best aspects of their trading as well as financial management strategies. This strategy will ensure that your previous strategies are effective and reliable. As the market is ever-changing and always changing the strategies you apply to your business will not remain the identical. This also allows you to adapt to changing markets.

If you don't have this plan without this strategy, you'll just being fumbling around. If you've got an effective method in place, it is possible to make cash, however it's not certain. Although you may earn money but it may not be the amount you could. What is the reason you would want to give up the possibility of earnings? In order to prevent such a thing from occurring, you must conduct an evaluation and optimization strategies.

The elements that make up Binary Options Strategies Three elements that are common to the strategies for trading binary options they are listed in the following order.

Step 1: Make signals

An indicator is a sign that the value of a particular asset is changing in a specific direction. Naturally, the prices of assets fluctuate constantly. You need an indicator that will predict the movement ahead of time. The signal is then created.

Two ways can be used for generating signals. First is using of news. The second is through technical analysis.

The creation of signals through messages is the most commonly used method particularly for beginners or novice binary option traders. This includes an analysis of the happenings in the media, e.g., announcing an organization, or announcing an industry's progress, and releasing government information on inflation. For many cases positive news indicates that the prices will increase, whereas negative news may cause loss of value.

The first step to implement this method knows what stories to anticipate seeing when. This is why you can find cheap calendars in the majority of top platform for trading in binary options. Being aware that the business's profit and loss accounts are due within two days allows you to schedule the analysis process and your trading activities for the region.

The top platforms also provide you with the information that you should look for in a news story. It is essential to understand the earnings report of a business must be filed within two days. It is more valuable if you understand what market expectations are for the earnings report. You can then decide what to include in your report's content and anticipate the contents and shifts in market prices. Also, you can make your decisions Based on market expectations and reactions following publication.

The news is positive that are part of the trading strategy and, most important of all, it's simple to grasp and evaluate. It has its own drawbacks. The most significant issue is the unpredictability of market conditions. A company, for instance, might release a profit loss report and indicate the increase in profits. The report could be a good news story on first glance, and generate a positive reaction in the market but the document might contain data that alarms investors. As an example, earnings aren't as great as expected. It could mean that the market is moving less than what was expected and, at times, in the opposite direction, causing prices to decline even if the event in question is deemed favorable.

It's difficult to know how long a movement is likely to take or how far it'll go. If you examine the case of the business's earnings statement, it is likely to have a positive outlook which means that the company's share values are expected to go up. However, how long will the process take when the price increase and at what point does the price hit a high point? This is a question that remains unanswered.

Trading based on the analysis of technical aspects provides an alternative. This method aims at predicting the development of prices for assets regardless of changes within the larger market.

It is all concerned with determining how much the price of an asset fluctuated through the years. From this information it's feasible to discern patterns through the price movement that can be predicted for the coming years.

Although it sounds like a challenge, the brain has been performing it every day; for instance, when you encounter a person who's warm and friendly, you'll probably predict good things during the course of your relationship. However when someone is discrete or rude and secluded, it can be difficult to anticipate problems when it comes to relationships. The reason you make these judgments is due to your experiences in creating relationships and meeting new people.

The analysis of technical aspects is like this. It examines the current condition of assets before deciding through experience if prices remain relatively stable or is declining or growing.

The understanding of technical terms and concepts may be difficult. However, the overall idea it is at the same time as the daily job of forecasting future outcomes from past experience.

The big question is: should you choose to use the method of message trading or the technique analysis approach? This is contingent on numerous variables, and the answers will differ for each person. The most effective advice is to determine which strategy is the best fit for your needs and also which makes the greatest profit. Naturally, it is not possible to try out strategies using your own hard-earned cash. However, there's a second option to use the demo account. Many reputable binary options trading platforms provide the possibility to open a demo account which allows you to utilize virtual cash to buy and sell binary options. This is and not the real thing. Demo accounts are not real money there is no chance to earn an income, but there is no loss of cash. It is possible to test your methods without risking any funds.

Another aspect to take into consideration when analyzing strategies and indicators is the focus on short-term. The purpose of investing strategies is to forecast the rate of change in the asset over a longer duration, for instance for a period of 10 years. The type of data isn't used in trading binary options. It is better to be aware of whether the price is likely to be moving in the next couple of minutes, hours or even the following day. Forecasting the price for 10 years will not be pertinent.

To do this, you require short-term indicators and strategies.

Step 2: How much do you need to make a trade?

In essence, it is an approach to managing money. The strategies vary in their the degree of complexity and effectiveness, beginning with the idea of generating an equal amount for every purchase. Martingale strategy and the percentage strategy are the other two strategies. To ensure long-term success then the latter strategy is the most effective.

The same amount of money into every single transaction is zero plans. This is a risky strategy since it fails to think about your overall profit as well as the total amount that you hold in your account. Both are vital elements that, if not taken into consideration could quickly drain your account balance.

Let's take a look at two additional general strategies. Let's start by Martingale's capital strategy.

The principal idea behind Martingale's strategy is to recuperate the losses as fast as is possible. That means, following the loss of a trade, massive quantities of cash must be reinvested in the transactions. In the case of example, you might get a fixed amount of your trade funds, which is doubled each time you lose. If you win then you'll be back to being successful, but not at the break-even point.

The problems with this strategy can arise when you lose multiple trades within a row. Every loss-making trade within the Martingale strategy is a sign of that you invest more money in the subsequent deal. This can add up fast. As an example, suppose there's a loss of 10 sales. It's quite a bit, yet this isn't an unreasonable or absurd situation. If you are losing 10 trades, the 11th trade should be at least 1024 times what you originally traded for you to remain in the Martingale method. There aren't any budgets that are able to endure such a rise, regardless of whether the price of your initial trade was not that high.

The issue is how precise the predictions you make are, and if you are able to prevent or reduce the loss of trades. It is essential to understand about binary trading and it isn't an exact science. Even trades that you're confident will work could result in loss. It is not uncommon to lose streaks, regardless of how proficient trading you may be. There is no way to know the best time to stop the loss. Thus, the Martingale financial management method is not a good choice for the majority of people.

The percentage method is more than risky and thus is popular with traders of all kinds and traders, particularly people who aren't familiar dealing with binary options. It's pretty straightforwardthat the amount you invest in the trade is contingent upon the amount of money in your account. If the transaction is lost and your balance on the account decline, decreasing the amount you invest for the subsequent transaction. However in the event that you are successful with a trade, the amount funds that you invest for the following trade will increase due to the fact that your account balance is higher.

This method helps maintain your cash balance in order to earn a consistent profit throughout time.

There is a question as to how much of your credit you would like to use. In general an investor who believes in that they are taking a risk could select a value of around five percent. A trader who doesn't like risks chooses around 2 percent.

Let's suppose that you decide to invest 5 percent of the balance of your account. For a $500 account then your transaction would cost just $25. If your balance decreases to $300, the investments will also drop. Each transaction costs you just $15. However, if your account balance grows by $800, then each of your transactions would cost you $40.

It is a method that will only allow you to spend the maximum amount you are able to be able to afford. This strategy is designed to maximize your profit and safeguard your cash flow when times are tough or you're on an unprofitable streak.

Step 3 - Improve your strategy

It is possible to do this through analyzing the results with an account book. It's an easy yet extremely effective idea. The idea is to keep a journal where you write down every transaction that you've completed. It is then possible to find patterns and trends to determine what is working as well as what isn't.

It is particularly effective when you're just beginning and striving to develop an effective method. In the case of this is to make trades using signal analysis and messages signals. An organized diary will help you separate these offers, so you are able to determine which are more beneficial. As an example, you could realize that you're earning double the value of transactions that you are receiving due to the technical analysis. However, from experience you're aware that you're spending much more time dealing with the messages of messages, rather than the technical analysis. Your journal suggests that you need to look at changing the way you strategy.

All depends on the deals that perform and which don't. The only method to accomplish this is keep track of the transactions and the trading diary can be a powerful instrument.

A trading journal is where it is possible to concentrate on specifics to improve the overall strategy of trading. At the end of the day you will reach a stage where you wish to improve your profit by a couple of percent. It's impossible to perform your job effectively without keeping excellent documents. However a successful conclusion to this process can bring an additional profit of hundreds or perhaps hundreds of thousands of dollars.

Be sure to utilize your trade journal to review the entirety of your approach to trading and not only your strategy for trading. It is important to know how you manage funds and also how to assess the amount of money you spend on each trade. It also includes determining the most beneficial value for your purchase, as well as the best style.

You can then explore the specifics. You can, for instance, determine the top days of the week and the most productive times during the day. This can assist you tailor your strategy. It is also possible to determine the brokers that work best for you as well as other information.

The trade journal will inform many things. The pressure of working with too many persons simultaneously time is a challenge. If you are doing this it is difficult to exactly what changes are beneficial and which are not. One of the easiest ways to address this issue is to pay attention to specific changes, study the effects of them, then move on. Also, keeping a trade diary is crucial to the process.

If you don't keep an account of your trade, you should start whenever you can. This becomes an essential instrument.

Strategies

In the case of binary options trading you have a wide range of options that you can choose from? The best and longest-running strategy to reduce risk however is to concentrate only on one particular asset You should only trade assets that you understand most well, like euro-dollar rates. Regular trading can help you become familiar with it and forecasting the direction of the value becomes more straightforward. Here are two kinds of strategies that are extremely beneficial in making use of binary option trading.

Strategy for a Trend

This is the most popular strategy used by novice and experienced traders. This method is frequently described as a bear-bull method and is focused on observing increasing and decreasing the line of flat trending the assets that can be traded. If a flat trendline is forecast, the cost of assets is likely to rise and it's suggested to make use of the option with no touching.

In the event that the trend line suggests that the asset is increasing choose CALL.

When the line of trend suggests that the investment is declining in value, then select PUT.

The method operates in exactly the same manner as the CALL/PUT choice, except it is possible to select the amount that the asset will not need to exceed the specified period. In this case, the Google stock value is $540. The platform for trading has a price of $570. There is no contact return is at 77 percent. If the price does not reach $570 by the set time the company earns gain.

Pinocchio Strategy

The strategy is utilized in situations where it is anticipated that the value of an investment will increase dramatically or change in a negative direction. If the value you are expecting to increase, use CALL. If it is anticipated to decrease then select

PUT. It is recommended to do this on the demo account of a broker's.

Straddle Strategy

Utilize this strategy whenever you are experiencing volatility in the market or just prior to the publication of significant news about certain stocks, or even the forecasts of analysts are in the air. This is a highly regarded method used by the international trading world. This technique is renowned as a way to not select the option PUT and CALL, but instead, placing them both on the asset of choice.

It is generally recommended to apply PUT when the worth of an asset is increasing however there are indications or reports that the value could soon decrease. If a change occurs, you can put the option CALL in the asset and anticipate that it will return to normal within a short time. The same can be accomplished with the opposite approach through the provision of CALL for sale at a bargain cost and increasing the value of the assets PUT. This increases the likelihood of success at the minimum one trading option which results "in the money." The straddle method is highly regarded by traders when markets fluctuate between rising and falling as well as when an investment has a high volatility.

Risk-reduction strategy

It is one of the most well-known strategies utilized from experienced traders of binary options across the globe. Its goal is to lower the possibility of risk in trading and improve the odds of success that results in a significant growth in profit. The strategy works using the PUT and CALL options in a different manner. This can be particularly useful when dealing with assets that have fluctuating prices. In reality the binary option can result in two outcomes. The simultaneous trading of two different forecasts with a single instrument will ensure that at the very least one is positive.

Hedging strategy

This method is generally called "pairing" which is typically employed together with investment firms, binary option companies and traditional exchanges in order to reduce and shield the potential risks. The strategy works through placing both the put and put in the identical asset. This guarantees that regardless of the direction taken by the price of the asset this transaction will result in an outcome that is successful. The investor will earn a gain "in the form of money." It can be a fantastic option to ensure your security as an investor in every circumstance. This is an security method to prepare the investor for all scenarios.

The fundamental analysis

The strategy is mainly used for stock trading, and more importantly, for traders who want to understand more about the assets they select. This improves their ability for predicting the price of future changes. This method requires a complete analysis of all firm's financials. It should contain income statements, financial statements, and market share information.

Chapter 9: Choosing Between a Call or Put Option

Binary options trading is different than the other kinds of trading however, that doesn't mean it isn't possible to make money working with these types of choices. Once you know the basics of trading binary options it is simple to trade and can be profitable as compared to other forms of transactions. There are many advantages to investing in binary options. When it comes to the amount of payout is concerned, there's an absolute middle-ground, in terms of gain or loss. Another thing to note is that the binary option market is one where you'll know exactly the potential profits and loss will be prior to when making a decision to trade.

The various analyses of statistics along with additional elements part of binary options trading. These help traders determine whether to use either a call option or put option to trade. Each binary option trade is tied to the movements of the price of the actual asset in the marketplace. When you put a call option, you're anticipating a decline in the price of the asset when you choose a call option then you're predicting the price of the asset will rise. In order to profit from trading in binary options, the worth of the asset in question needs to be at or below the strike price of either a put or call option at the time when the expiration date of the option.

This is why it is crucial that traders be able to accurately predict market situations when making a trade. The market could be either bearish or bullish. If the market is believed to be bullish then it's a good time to make purchases. When that happens, people seem to believe that prices will increase. A market that is bearish however is the complete opposite of a bearish one and the general trend of the market is downward and prices will begin to fall rapidly.

One of the main reasons why binary options trading have been deemed as a popular option is because traders are able to gain from a decrease or an increase in price of the market. The importance of statistical analysis is for traders to think about prior to making an offer. A statistical analysis will allow you to determine the best entry points for the trade as well as its cost performance. If you find that prices are moving in the right direction, it should be easy to make the trade. If you don't have a reliable indicator, it is best to make your decision by looking at the past price movements.

Also, you must consider expiration time elements when deciding to make the binary option trade. Statistics will reveal the low and high prices the asset has touched during the course of a certain time. Even though the asset could exceed the limits set by the study, it'll generally stay within the limits.

Many experienced traders consider that when the price of the asset being traded closer to a certain point in the statistical range then the next event that is likely to occur over the next few days will be a change in trend. The most likely time to make either a put or call option is nears the time. When you are able to speculate on the value of an asset and push the limits that you could be successful in trading; However, keep in mind that they aren't easy to determine because price fluctuations tend to stay within the bounds.

It is not advisable to base an option to call or put choice solely on speculation. If this is the case, and your choice isn't supported by actual evidence or numbers and facts, you may be tempted to put off trading because the odds of success are very low.

Chapter 10: Objectives for Beginners Binary Traders

Goals are essential not just for starting out with trading as a trader, but also throughout your career as an investor. In setting goals, traders are prone to making typical mistakes, which often steer to them straying from their route. In this post we will discuss certain goals a new trader needs to achieve and that these goals are thought as important.

Learning Goals vs. Performance Goals

It is essential to be able distinguish between an objective for performance from the goal of learning. Learning goals are about taking action as well as understanding when it is not appropriate to act. The goal of performance is measuring the effectiveness of every action. If you are a beginner in trading I recommend that education goals should take precedence over goals for performance.

A performance-based goal such as "I would like to make $1,000 per day from trading" will result in a low results. Instead, establishing a learning objective that is based on an act such as "I am going to carefully evaluate every signal that I get and then manage these in line with my own strategy for trading" is the best goal.

A commitment to follow the plan in all instances is vital in order to develop solid trading habits. Thus, it's best to use a sound trading plan in good circumstances rather than worrying about results. If you follow your plan, results will be the same. Therefore the main goal should be adhering to your trading strategy.

Consistency

In the beginning, test it for a few days or just stick with one trade and before moving on to the next and up to. Your goal is "My intention is to make trades only if I get a valid trade signal, and only upon those signals do I make a trade." You can then prolong it for two consecutive days, and then three, four and then further. Be sure to create basic rewards or sanctions when you don't adhere to or fail to follow your strategy. This method of setting targets is successful over the long term.

These goals will help you develop an environment of consistency. It is crucial to be consistent when you are trying to be successful in trading. It is a result of having a habit that are formed, and when you develop an effective trading routine increases your chance to become a successful trader. It can be somewhat difficult to be steady because the conditions for trading change each day. To prevent any issues then you must set your goals as I have mentioned in the previous paragraph.

New Beliefs

In some instances, your mind may not allow you to make the right choices so you could make mistakes. Another goal you should set for yourself is the setting of up new mental beliefs which will keep you focused. The trick is to build new belief systems by repeatedly informing yourself and making yourself believe these beliefs and stop your brain from forming doubts.

Here are some ideas you should strive to develop:

If I adhere to the plan I have made, I'm not the sole one to decide how much I can expect to earn. Trading strategies and market's conditions decide my capability to make. Therefore, I am able to remove any doubts or false beliefs and believe in my trading strategies that I intend to implement.

I'll judge myself on whether I adhered to my plan or not, and not upon the amount I earn. Some days, I may make a decent amount, but that's not sufficient because I missed an opportunity to earn even more but there will occasions when earning one dollar is enough, even if economic conditions are very unfavourable.

I'm not able to know what's going to occur, but relying on anything other than what I have planned will hinder my plans to achieve success. Everything can go wrong within the world of finance. That's why it's important adhere to my strategy, as it is effective.

In light of the preceding concept, I realize that I don't have to predict what's coming up to earn a profit. It is enough to stick with my rules and exercise an element of confidence.

As the markets are active, I have to establish a loss limit in each transaction I enter. In addition, I have to make sure that the risk I take is a tiny portion of my amount of investment.

Putting it All Together

If you've a goal to improve your skills, then the it will result in performance as a consequence from this plan. As a beginner you must aim to identify a trading method and adhere to the plan. If you are unable to come across a strategy which you like so you can create your own. As you create your strategy, be sure that the plan you have created is legitimate and that it works to your advantage for a long time. Be sure to stick to your plan during trading, and then for two trades, and then for a whole day, for a week or so. Do not worry about your performance as your main goal is to establish the regularity. If the method you choose doesn't work and you aren't sure what to do, make the needed changes and then start over. If the plan does work out but you not able to implement it, make sure you establish the values you mentioned in this paragraph and stick to the goals you set.

Set goals can give you the motivation needed to continue. It helps you evaluate the progress you make as an investor.

Chapter 11: Getting Started

In this article we will discuss the steps you could follow in order to start your journey with trade in binary options.

Step One: Pick a Strategy

In the preceding sections in the previous sections, you learned about various strategies for trading binary options. Spend your time to test whether these strategies are a good fit well for you, or not. Verify the efficiency and effectiveness of these strategies. Additionally, you can combine multiple indicators into your personal strategy. Below are some indicators you could take into consideration:

Price levels

Trends

Candlestick patterns

Chart patterns

Moving average indicator

Fibonacci levels

On-chart indicators

Area indicators

There are many other indicators to consider--there are many others and all of them work in different ways. The key is to pair the signals of different indicators to decrease the chance of receiving a poor indicator and increase odds to your advantage.

Step Two: Calculate the Returns

We will assume that your payout is 80% and that you are liable for 100% of the money which you put in. The ratio between profits and losses is 8:10. What is your plan be? And what should you consider to determine the break-even level? Consider that you execute approximately 100 trades a day, and you invest $10 for each trade. This implies that your investment totals $1000. If your method achieves a success rate of 55 percent percentage, then you're likely to be able to win around 55 of 100 trades you take. If your prediction is correct the odds are that you'll win the amount of $8. If the prediction proves wrong, you'll be losing 10 dollars. If it is proven the possibility of winning around 55 trades the profit you earn is $440 ($8 multiplied by 55). The loss in contrast would be the sum of $450 ($10 for losing 45 trades).

The method you chose for doesn't pay off because you'll end up making losing $10.

Another test is available with identical conditions - 80 percent payback The success rate of the method is 70. If you take 100 trades using this method, you could win around 70 trades while losing 30. Thus, your gain for this scenario would be $560 ($8 for 70 trades that are successful) Your loss is $300 ($10 per 30). So, your net profits will be $260.

You can take time time to study the return you can expect from various strategies, based on past data you have and pick one you believe to be lucrative.

Step Three: Money Management

When you are trading, it is important to never overlook the possibility of the possibility of luck. If you make a deposit of $100 to your account for trading and then spend $20 every day, your odds of losing are quite high because you will not be able to take on more than 5 consecutive losses (the chance of it being the case is very extremely high). The best advice is that you have enough money in your account in order to be able to execute at least 100 transactions. What is the chance of being able to lose 100 times in a row? Pretty not likely, isn't it? The process is similar as flipping a coin. It's either tails or heads however it isn't exactly the same 100 times.

Step Four: Select a Binary Options Broker

It is important to pay focus on a few factors when selecting an agent. There are many scammers that will not let you cash out your funds So, do your investigation. A reputable broker

Always regulated and adheres to the rules of the country.

Is around for some time. Scam brokers usually get in the span of a couple of years.

Have favorable online reviews. What have previous clients and customers saying about a broker? Review the reviews thoroughly.

We will always provide an array of trading instruments. It's not a good idea to limit yourself to just five currency pairs when trading Do you?

It has a user-friendly interface.

Included are various indicators of trading to assist with analysis and design of a profitable trading plan.

Step Five: Establish and fund your account

If you've got your financial affairs in order, this will be the simplest process. You must follow the regulations for your brokerage service for establishing your account. It is necessary to verify your identity as a person, confirm your identity, verify your account and after that, you are able to deposit funds to your account. Make sure you adhere to the guidelines for managing money mentioned in the article. Make sure to keep the balance on your account as small as is possible at first. When you become trader, you may boost this balance.

Step Six: Executing Your First Trade

Once you're ready and you have transferred your money in the account, begin by investing just one percent of each trade you take. Then, you will have to adjust your investment per trade according in the amount you choose. Choose the time of expiry time interval of the binary option. Conduct your study with care and adhere to the plan you have chosen. If you find that the price is likely to rise you can choose to take an option to call, but when the price falls you can opt for the put option.

Binary options can be quite ingenuous and offer the most simple investments available to be found. They have rules that are straightforward to learn and the risk that comes with them is low. However, you must adhere to the tested and tried techniques and regulations for becoming an expert trader. It is essential to develop solid strategies for trading and manage your money and think strategically whether you'd like to be prosperous.

Chapter 12: Things to Consider While Selecting a Broker

It is essential to evaluate various brokers prior to choosing one. It doesn't matter if you're beginning to trade in the very first time or are an existing professional in the field, you must choose the best broker for you. It's difficult to locate a trustworthy and trustworthy broker from the many thousands of brokers that are available in the present. If you have made up that you want to trade it is essential to take the initial couple of days researching, comparing and finally, settling on a suitable broker to trade binary options with. A few brokers give solid advice on trading, however there are others who focus on making profit to themselves. In this part we will discuss various aspects should be considered when choosing the binary options broker.

Image Courtesy of Pixabay

Compare the Deposit Bonus

The majority of brokers give a welcome or deposit bonus. It is important to evaluate the amounts offered by various brokers and find one with the most favorable bonus. There are some that aren't offering any bonuses However, they provide an affordable deposit. For those who are brand unfamiliar with binary trading must select a broker offering an initial deposit that is low. It is possible to increase the amount of your deposit once you're at ease. Keep in mind the terms and conditions can be combined in any bonus brokers offer. If you believe that the terms don't align with your plan for trading make sure you do not choose to accept the bonus. Additionally, ensure that you take the time to study all terms and conditions that the broker outlines, including the fine print prior to selecting one.

Payout Percentage

There are many platforms that permit customers to receive minimum five or 10 percent returns. their return ranges from 75 to 90 percent. This is contingent on the platform you choose. Therefore, you'll need take your time reading the various details regarding all of these and choose one who can provide the most lucrative payouts while also offering fair rates of service.

Minimum Deposit

Nearly all brokers meet this requirement prior to allowing a trader begin trading. The next step is to look to find a broker that is within your financial budget. You can have a few options in case the features and advantages offered are impressive. If you're only beginning to learn about trading, it's recommended to go to go with a broker that offers the option of an initial deposit of a certain amount.

Deposit and Withdrawal

Certain brokers demand an initial deposit of a certain amount along with an amount of withdrawal per transaction. If you'd like to be able to trade, you must avoid being restricted by these restrictions. When you make any transaction you want to do be sure that you have your required balance, instead of making the transaction in the way you prefer.

Multiple Assets Investing

The kind of assets provided by brokers can differ. Some may provide two assets, while other could have more than three. Always select a platform which includes more assets. The more options offered, the more the possibilities to trade diverse markets. If you are looking to boost your margins of profit, all should be your primary focus is investing in diverse kinds of investments. The idea is to diversify your portfolio in order to reduce risks. If it is feasible and you are able to do so, you'll be capable of investing in stocks, commodities as well as Forex in a single transaction. It's a great idea to maintain a varied and balanced portfolio. It's a smart idea not to throw all your eggs into one basket.

Trading Tools

Some trading platforms have a range of tools for trading including indicators, signals as well as automated signals. However, certain platforms do not offer of these tools. The majority of brokers provide automated trading services however a few of them work with binary options robots from other companies in this regard. Choose an option that is compatible with its tools. They make the work as a trader simpler, but if are just beginning to learn about trading, then you'll require every assistance is available.

Demo Account

It's always good to have a few hours of trading knowledge before you begin trading. The most effective option in your arsenal is to begin by using an account that is demo. After you've gained the information about the way binary options work and the various types of options and numerous strategies that you are able to employ, the next thing is to experiment with the strategies. With an account that is demo, you can gain an experience firsthand of how live markets function without having to expose your self to the dangers of trading in trading in a live market. These services on demo accounts and how they function are very like the way in the way live markets operate. Certain demo accounts can only be used for a short period of time, while others offer lifetime services. While you're practicing trading techniques along with techniques, it's crucial to select a lifetime demo account. It is essential to become familiar with all aspects of binary options. if you do not, it's going to be a challenge to stay afloat in a highly competitive market.

Image Courtesy of Pixabay

Customer Service

The most effective way to find out about the quality of service the brokerage platform provides is to go through the feedback, reviews as well as testimonials from other clients and users. This can be done with an easy Google search. This will allow you to determine the ratings of users on the brokerage platform. In addition to the score, you'll get some details about how many previous customers found that particular platform useful and if they're meeting the commitments that they have made. Additionally, it is the perfect way to check the credibility of a brokerage platform.

User Interface

The platform must be simple to use. If it's difficult to operate and features complicated navigation systems, it will be difficult to navigate it. It's not just an unnecessary effort and time, it could result in unnecessary waste of time also.

Therefore, it's essential to ensure that the platform you choose is easy for users. When you've made your list of possible platforms you be interested in You must then test each one on your own using demo accounts.

Expiry Dates

Certain brokers let you make trades expire in several days or hours, but other brokers may have rigid rules on expiry dates which stipulate that you have to be patient for some days after your trade is completed. Be sure to think about these aspects before you choose the broker. Review their the terms and conditions prior to you choose a broker.

Early Exit

A few brokers provide traders with the possibility of exiting an investment prior to the expiry date. Other brokers may be extremely specific about when you must remain until when the trade expires. Always select a broker that provides an exit option. In the event that, at the close of the period expiring what you get is loss, it's best to quit when you notice difficulty and stop the losses right then rather than extending it. So, you're able to limit any loss you may endure. Consider it an option to control damage.

Multiple Languages

It's a good idea when a trader is able to find an online brokerage that can support several languages. With the advent of technology, where there is no physical barrier to trade, it can be a bit disappointing not being able to trade due to a lack of a language. Make sure that the trading platform you choose can be used in different languages. Broker services must be able to accommodate your preferred language, otherwise it could be difficult to use and navigate an online platform using an language that you don't understand.

If you want to be successful in the trading of binary options you must find the appropriate broker. It is among the main aspects to consider when trading. Prepare yourself to invest an amount of time to think about this, and don't think you can find a top broker at the first attempt. If you don't have an concept of all the aspects you must be aware of before choosing one, it may make it difficult to pick the right one. Use all of the info which I've gave in this article to help you decide which broker to choose. Selecting an unlicensed unsafe, insecure, or unregulated broker is bound to cause troubles for the client. Avoid all the hassle.

Chapter 13: What are Binary Options?

Achieving success in trading binary options involves being aware of how an option operates and also the potential changes in the price of that asset on which the option is built. Like the term "binary" indicates that these types of options are profitable or ineffective based on only two scenarios that include the value of the asset being traded upwards or downwards. An investor must be aware of the possibility of price fluctuations at some point in the near future, regardless of whether the investment is a commodity or a index of the stock market, the company stock, or some other product with quantifiable features.

It also implies that binary options can yield an undetermined return for a trader, or none at all. The seller of the option (i.e. the broker) and the trader come to an agreement in the conditions that determine the amount of profit or loss that will be made prior to the trade is made from the broker.

The simplicity and Binary "win either way" result make binary option trading possible for any sensible investor. Risks and rewards are clearly stated from the beginning. The outcome is determined by whether traders' prediction of changes (up or downwards) of value is accurate. This is quite a difference when compared with other kinds of investments which we'll soon be able to discover.

Although the concepts may seem easy, there are some specific words that are used by dealers and traders for describing binary options trades. They are the most commonly used, Put and Call, refer to what a traders anticipate as a potential change in the price of the asset. If there is a belief for the asset's price to drop then the trader would purchase an option called a Put. If, on the other hand, it is expected that the value of the product will rise then the buyer will purchase an option called a Call. Additional terms are also available however, these are the easiest and most widely utilized.

In addition to determining whether the asset will increase or decrease in value another crucial aspect is to establish the time duration that the binary option trade is expected to be. What happens to the price during the time frame has no impact on the result of the majority of trading in binary options (although there are some "exotic" choices where it can be relevant). In the majority of cases it's the final value of the assets at the time that the time the period ends that's the decisive element. The duration is decided prior to when the trade begins and is not altered after the trade has begun.

The predetermined time period signifies that there's a major difference between binary options trading along with other financial products, like share market securities. Investors who purchase shares want that the cost of the shares to increase in order that could then trade the shares and earn profits. However, there is no obligation that an investor sells shares at one particular time and they can be kept for a long time. If, in addition, prices of shares falls during the time, investors suffer losses for at most until the time when the value goes back to a profit price.

Binary option trades however operate strictly in accordance with the expiry date that is predetermined for the contract. A three-day contract implies you that your binary options transaction expires three days following the date it begins. The traders earn profit based on the reliability of their initial estimates. If they purchased a one-week Put option for oil and oil's price decreased at the close of that week, the investors could earn a profit.

In accordance with the terms by the broker who sells the option, buyers are able to select the time of expiration to suit their personal preferences for trading. In order to facilitate fast turnover of trades in which contracts are closed and opened in a relatively short time, binary option expiration dates are usually available in a range of 1 min to one day. The above range, which spans between 1 day and seven days, for example is a medium-term trading. The long-term trading option is offered for time periods that vary from a week up to one month.

The way a trader selects the various expiry dates that are available is based on the individual's preferences in trading as well as individual plans for trading. Regardless of the option, planning in advance is crucial in the application of a sound method that has been tried under real-world conditions prior to investing cash on options.

Binary Options trader also benefit because there aren't any commissions or fees for trading to pay and there are the spread cost is not a problem. They can seriously eat away at profit margins and turn an effective Forex or trading stock strategy to a loss, however it's not something should be worried about.

Losing or winning on the binary options can be measured through the smallest difference between the beginning price of an asset as well as its value after the expiration date of the contract. Contrary to shares where winners and losses are each made bigger and less so but binary options don't make use of the amount of the variance. A small percentage difference can result in a win or loss with a binary contract however, the amount to be that is won or lost stays identical, regardless of whether the value of the asset changes a tiny or significant amount.

Chapter 14: Types of Binary Options bet

One of the major advantages for those who trade in binary option is the fact that there's not a requirement to keep and handle the asset that is used as the basis. An option in binary that utilizes gold as an investment for instance does not require traders to own the gold at anytime time. It is an enormous simplification and allows trading in binary options for commodities the same as stocks market indexes, currencies or a similar base asset. In contrast the binary options contracts have more flexibility, in the form of increasingly exaggerated "touch" option.

Binary Option "Touch" Trades

Four "touch" options that follow let traders design their trades much in a more precise manner than simply calling or putting options. The concept of "touch" is the value of an asset fluctuating in a certain amount (up and down). The fundamental principles of the binary option will not change. Whether the price has been reached or it doesn't. the trader makes either an agreed-upon profit or loses the amount of money paid for this binary option.

One-Touch. The trader forecasts that the price of an asset will be at a specific threshold during the contract. When this price is attained and the trader is successful, then he will receive the option payment.

No-Touch. The trader forecasts that the value of an asset won't attain a specific amount. Payments could differ depending on the market value as it is when the contract begins and to the trigger price set and larger variations (making "no-touch" much more probable) will result in smaller payments.

Double One-Touch. The trader believes the price will change however, they aren't sure what they are going to be, whether upwards or down. This is where both an upper and a lower trigger price will be set. When the price increases or drops to the value of the one or both trigger price, the buyer receives the payment.

Double No-Touch. This is the reverse of Double One-Touch option can be lucrative for the investor if neither the the lower trigger prices are met.

The variety of options listed above allows traders to modify their investments in binary options in accordance with the current market conditions. Markets that are highly volatile, for instance could be handled making use of Double One-Touch binary options to maximize the possibility of taking advantage of price movements that go that are either downwards or upwards. The markets that have a flat structure where price fluctuations could be both ways, but only in a narrow range will be best suited for double or no-touch binary choices.

It is essential to evaluate risk in a manner that is appropriate. The economic environment can trigger unexpected price fluctuations for assets. Technological issues related to the behavior of traders or shifts in the volume of market transactions could also trigger an unusual pattern of price movement.

If you are considering the alternatives mentioned above there's a second element that needs to be taken into account. What is it the case that "touch" (or "no-touch" option applicable based on the events in the course of the contract? or based on the circumstances following the expiration of the contract? The differences between the two scenarios is due to the so-called American and European fashion options, respectively.

A American type option analyzes the events that occur during the duration of the contract. Once the trigger price has been reached and the binary option has been executed with the associated gains or losses for the investor. As an example, suppose that for the One-Touch binary option when the value of the asset is at the trigger value just half way during the period of option and the option has been executed and the trader receives the amount.

An European type option analyzes what is happening at the time that the entire option ends. In the previous scenario in which the value of the asset has reached the trigger value at the time it is the trader who receives the money. But, if the value reached the trigger price at some point, and then was able to return to the initial price prior to the time of expiration the trader will not receive a pay out for the investor.

The decision to choose between American styles or European styles of contracts can depend on factors like reinvestment options (for example, when taking the option out immediately or in the future, then placing the funds elsewhere) as well as interest rates.

Avoiding Binary Option Scams

Achieving consistent success in trading binary options is a matter of proper strategy and preparation. Though this is easily accessible to many people, there's no quick way to become rich and, if there was no way to do so, everybody would be wealthy! The basic logic of this should have enough reason to make investors more cautious when it comes to binary options trading programs that claim to as easy to make money. Human nature frequently makes people believe their own desires, instead of what is actually happening.

But, the work involved to approach binary option trading correctly has several advantages. It allows traders to perceive the binary options market as simple financial instruments and stay away from the unfamiliarity that can surround trading. Additionally, it gives traders the chance to plan toward a positive outcome and maximizing profits and not having to depend on luck or intuition (both very unpredictable when it comes to trading with options).

Chapter 15: Placing Your First Binary Options Bet

The very first thing you have to choose prior to placing a bet is what asset you'll trade. Although it's obvious that an option must have an asset for it to even exist choosing the appropriate kind of option can be not as clear. The successful trade of options is one that makes the most of market conditions. Prices for assets can fluctuate depending on the time of day and shifting conditions; therefore, it's essential to find the appropriate asset at the appropriate time.

That means you must have an elementary grasp of the asset type which will be the basis for the trading. Without it, long-term achievement in trading binary options is not likely to be achieved from. Understanding of marketplace forces and timeframes are essential in determining the date of expiry time of the option. The combination of data will allow you to determine the chance of earning gain. A higher chance is, the greater amount of risk traders make; and in the opposite direction, a lower likelihood implies a less costly expenditure.

At a lot of trading sites it is possible to select the currency, time of expiration and the amount of trading is then automated to generate data on the amount that is to be made or won or lost. The next step, if you like the trading option will be to select "Buy" and follow your transaction until expiry time for the end outcome.

The only two possible outcomes that are possible (win and lose) can be determined prior to the time a binary option is executed, you are able to model your results with precision. The amount you lose the most is the cost of the option you purchased while your greatest profit is determined by the amount that is displayed by the trading station. The other investment products don't provide this level of assurance. Equity markets are one of them. The price of shares fluctuates which is why the amount of profit or loss investors can earn. If the situation is not favourable it is possible that all investment be lost if the business wassuing shares went under.

The ABC of Binary Options

The final outcome, winning or losing, from trading in binary options is dependent entirely on the direction an option price takes - it is not based on the quantity it is moved. This fundamentally alters the idea about the reliability of forecasts when compared with other financial instruments such as shares, like shares, for instance. Investments in shares are defined by the quantity by that the price fluctuates and the return on binary option trading isn't affected with small or large price fluctuations. It is only important that the price is moving in the direction you forecasted.

A potential return on trading binary options can be expressed in terms of an amount of percentage return. The rate of 80 per percent means that, if your trade succeeds, you get the price you paid to purchase your binary option and an additional 20. In the example above for a scenario, if you purchase the binary option for $100, and you are able to predict the direction the price is moving then your payment will equal $100 plus 80x 100: which is you will receive a total of $180. If you did not correctly predict that direction, you'll be unable to recover your investment of $100.

Certain brokers will offer rebates on failed trades (up up to 20% in certain cases) This helps pay for sudden price shifts.

The binary option market doesn't require investors to incur additional costs or commissions for the trade. It is not necessary to take into account the expense of spreads. Spreads are a factor that is a part of Forex transactions which can cause the trader to suffer net losses, even if the rate of exchange for the currency selected changed in the direction predicted by trader. The profit and loss structures are transparent. Traders can see prior to trading the exact amount they could win or lose.

Brokers have also made efforts to enhance trading including rebates previously mentioned. They have also helped facilitate all aspects of trading with trading platforms that are designed to simplify the whole process and available to investors as well as new and solo traders.

Chapter 16: Money Management & Position Sizing

Postition Sizeing Deals - How the majority of your account is at risk for every trade. This is why it's an essential aspect of trading since when you are risking too much it is possible to lose the majority or all of your accounts in the event of a string of poor trading. In contrast, if you do not put your money at risk, your account won't grow in any way.

In the case of regular trading in Forex, Stocks, etc. This is a difficult process to decide on the size of a position due to the fact that the risk of every trade isn't predetermined as it is with binary options. Since we know precisely what we are likely to make or lose from every bet, it becomes more simple.

Before deciding on how much of our accounts we're taking on we must first figure out how much the total amount we will contribute to the binary options account.

Certain brokers allow you to start by putting in as little as 100 dollars. I'd recommend a minimal of $500 because a sensible way of sizing positions requires the use of small amount cash for each trade. So if you have only $100, the account would increase in size so slow that it will just barely worth it. Naturally, beginning with an initial amount, and later depositing more money to build your account to an impressive amount is a smart plan, especially if are new to the game: better not to commit any errors on smaller accounts than on a big one.

I also suggest to have an account with 2 binary option brokers, and then split your profits across the two. There are several reasons to do this. Most importantly brokers may cease to exist with no warning. You certainly don't want your money tied to the same broker in the event of that happening. Furthermore, each broker has various strengths and weaknesses; and pricing may be distinct between one broker and the one.

For setting the size of your positions, the easiest, and my personal opinion ideal - method is to risk just an amount from your balance on every trade.

In the example above, if your balance was $500 and you planned to take a risk of 10% that's why you'd make sure that the option you purchased would be less risky than $50. I wouldn't recommend taking the risk more than 10% at the very least, in the beginning. The 10% rate is already greater than the other kinds of trading, and your chance of ruin is too excessive if you go any more.

When you've got plenty of trading transactions There are different ways you could determine what the best risk-to-reward ratio is, analysing your percent precision, the risk of a loss and also calculating the "Kelly value" However, considering all the effort involved this model, it is a tough one to beat.

Four Steps to Profitable Trading

1. Do not trade based on your intuition or on a whim. Choose any of the strategies which you are fully aware of and follow them

2. Select the bet type that is appropriate (Call/Put or Touch/No-Touch) and then expiration date, for the strategy.

3. Pick your broker carefully is sure to stay clear of the risk of having your entire money at one place

4. Do not ignore effective managing your money. It might appear boring, but if don't pay attention and you suffer many losing

trades, the money you spent are likely to disappear.

Your First Binary Options Strategy

The most efficient way to ensure a successful trader in binary options is to make an use of the power of technology for monitoring the trends. Fundamental analysis (the analysis of economic as well as financial data) is not very useful when it comes to trading binary options, since it's focused on longer durations of time rather than those used by binary option traders.

The trend-based method monitors the major shifts in the price, be it upwards or downwards, and determines the direction of the price change using call options or put option.

The previous history of a individual entity is what can tell a trader about the future direction of price changes of the company is most likely to take. If the price change is continuing at the same rate for a set time the change can be regarded as an ongoing trend. When it comes to binary options, this period of time could be anywhere between one hour and the duration of a month or even longer.

Additionally, there are the trends that are within trends. For instance, short length trends form an element of larger, more global trends, which can extend for as many as months. Every decision regarding trading must be based on both long and short trending trends. The Forex market will understand the rationale behind this however, binary option traders must be following suit as well.

Simpler than that they are essentially two kinds of market developments:

In the time sequence in question both the highs in position and lows in the positional range have a higher closing price than the preceding ones. The most common changes will upward trend, even if there remains certain negative pullbacks in the price movement.

The above diagram shows an upward trend with the horizontal red line that runs diagonally from in the direction of left and right.

The simplest definition of a downtrend is that it's essentially opposite of the upward trend. Positional highs and lows are both less than their predecessors, when we are moving along the horizontal time line. In the opposite direction of the trend, reverse price movement (upwards in this case) and consolidation are likely, but generally the price is likely to decrease.

The above diagram illustrates a diagonal downward to indicate the downward trend.

Although disclaimers consistently state that future performance can't always be predicted from previous results and that monitoring the moving averages of an asset traded may be a good method of observing trends, by identifying the previous changes in direction of price.

The statistical benefits that are realized using a trend tracking method is used correctly can surpass any losses that occur because of the information provided by the strategy will never provide 100% accuracy. Because the historical price of assets is typically available for free on the in-house charting application or any other this strategy can be used for traders of all levels, novices or experts.

Support and Resistance Levels

Being aware of where resistance and support levels are helps to track patterns.

Support levels provide the lower limit at that price, which does not fall. It is a sign of where traders are buying and is because they believe that prices won't fall more than the level at which they are.

The resistance level provides an upper limit above that point, where price doesn't increase. If this is the case it is the general view of the investors is that the price won't increase much more. In contrast when a price "breaks out" by moving over the threshold of resistance, positioning price tends to go in that direction too.

The diagram below shows that the price dropped four time (shown by the arrows with four) until it reached a lowest before increasing once more and forming the level of support depicted. In the same way, it climbed twice until it reached an all-time high, prior to a decrease, which helped create the resistance threshold.

The levels of support and resistance that are applied to every part of a line trend show the way prices move at several points, and create precise pivot areas. These are helpful when markets are slow and more unpredictable during lower volume of activity, like for instance, during the night. It is also possible to use them for any other time duration.

Spotting Trends

The "moving average" indicator is the most efficient method to identify the direction of a movement, by providing an average rate of change for the price in a certain time period. Ten-day indicators show how much price changes for a time period of 10 days, as an example.

The calculation of moving averages is performed in various methods. In the case of the binary option, it might be useful to determine an average that takes recently-changed prices into account in addition to older price changes. This is how the "Exponential Moving Average" (aka EMA) does this. It is also known as the "Simple Moving Average" (the SMA), which doesn't apply other weighting system, is a different option, and SMA as well as EMA could be then comparably.

Some traders come across a way to identify trend patterns that are effective for time periods of an half an hour or more. A time span of one day is usually the best option due to greater precision and clarity of trend patterns in price action, as well as being less dependent on price swings that are temporary ("noise"). Longer periods than a day are less likely to be successful in being able to recognize trends promptly.

The trend can also be instantly altered by economic news as well as other announcements. The schedule of news announcements allows for a planned pause for trading to be scheduled so that traders do not take unwarranted risks.

Monitoring changes over a period of a day (intra-day) in binary options may result in 60-85 percent of the trades have been successful. If every trade is for identical amounts and the trades are all for the same amount, then trading is likely to yield a profit in the long run. The possibility of success for the strategy is in line with the price movement that is common to binary options. Improved judgment and skills improve the likelihood of success and profits. Also, it is a good alternative to the strategy that is based on a completely random selection between the sole two possibilities for a binary option.

Chapter 17: The Cup and Handle Pattern

This strategy for trading binary options was initially devised by William O'Neal for the stock market. He discussed this chart pattern called "cup and handle" with great detail in "How to make money in Stocks" the 1988 bestseller.

The main event that is portrayed by the pattern of a handle and cup is the emergence of a bullish price. This is the reason that we do not discuss Call options within this.

Two elements create the shape of the handle and cup:

A) In the first place, we have the cup. This is a rounded pattern that, like its name implies that is designed to look like an actual cup. It is composed of three areas of support for price at different levels that are horizontally joined by a curved line. There are at minimum two levels of resistance that could be joined to form the lid that is horizontally placed on the cup. It starts in the same area that is left, which is where the cup's beginning.

B) Then, there's the handle. The handle is a region which is immediately following the cup. Nearly similar trend lines follow the highs and lowers of the candles, in order to display a relatively little Retracement. Near the end of this post it is possible to see an example graphically of this pattern of handle and cup drawn in a chart.

After the handle, and the price movement it represents an upward breakout of the value of the asset then takes place which leads to a positive trend in the following days that can be seen in this pattern on the chart.

Trading With the Cup & Handle

The method of cup and handle for binary options is to do both of these:

A) Properly making the correct map of the handle and cup pattern.

B) Trading a call option based on the information contained from the chart pattern.

The manual process of tracing the pattern takes time, because it isn't always evident visually. One possible point of entry is the area of resistance created by candles. From there it is possible to observe not just the horizontal line separating two or more resistance points, as well as the curve that turns down and around beneath these points. The ideal balance for a such curve is one that's not that shallow, so it looks like a saucer instead of a cup. It is not too deep.

When the shape of the cup as well as its lid is determined, the handle must be identified. Because it's the region that consolidates price follows the handle, it is constructed from a line connecting the highs of the candle and another that joins the candle's lows. The handle could be in pennant or a flag form, but the flag is preferred.

Doing the Deal

The process of trading using an Call option is now initiated by a price rise by following the right map of the cup as well as the pattern of the handle. The breakout occurs at the top of the pennant or flag on the handle. This is followed by the candle pushed across the handle's upper line and closes higher than the handle line.

Because of the bullish nature this price action, and also the pattern it precedes is why using the Call option is your only option to trade. If breakout does occur (beware of fake outs) Make the Call option trade prior to the time of candle's opening which is immediately following the the breakout of the price. This chart shows the following:

The chart provides a simple illustration of how the chart design of the cup as well as handle could lead to trade. The equation of the curvature of the lid and cup which connects those points of resistance is a good fit with perfectly with the development of price movement. Handle follows next and is in these instance pennant patterns, with both trend lines narrowing slightly in relation to one another. Following the breakout, which is followed by the long candle to the right of the handle the price action then goes moving upwards. The option to buy Call is bought at the time that the candle next opens following the breakout candle's long one.

In this case the chart for a 4 hour period of EURAUD was employed. This means that an interval of between 8 and 12 hours should be considered to allow for the expiry time so that there is enough flexibility for the trading to earn a profit. Similar to that using an hourly chart could mean many days before the trade expiry time.

There is also the option to sell Touch as well as No Touch options. This is because that area beneath the cup is where the goal price for a no Touch option could be determined. The price target for an Touch option will be set a bit higher than the handle. The decision on whether or not these options can be pursued alongside those of the call option is entirely up to the individual trader.